Just Testify

Dr. J. Ortega

Just Testify

Copyright © 2020 by Dr. J. Ortega

All rights reserved. No part of this book may be reproduced or transmitted in any form or by any means without written permission of the author.

ISBN: 978-0-578-93186-9

Scripture marked (KJV) is taken from the King James Version of the Bible.

Scripture marked (NIV) is taken from THE HOLY BIBLE, NEW INTERNATIONAL VERSION®, NIV® Copyright © 1973, 1978, 1984, 2011 by Biblica, Inc.® Used by permission. All rights reserved worldwide.

Scripture marked (NKJV) is taken from the New King James Version®. Copyright © 1982 by Thomas Nelson. Used by permission. All rights reserved.

Scripture marked (NASB) is taken from the NEW AMERICAN STANDARD BIBLE®, Copyright © 1960, 1962, 1963, 1968, 1971, 1972, 1973, 1975, 1977, 1995 by The Lockman Foundation. Used by permission.

Scripture marked (NRSV) is taken from the New Revised Standard Version Bible, copyright © 1989 the Division of Christian Education of the National Council of the Churches of Christ in the United States of America. Used by permission. All rights reserved.

Scripture marked (AMP) is taken from the Amplified Bible, Copyright © 2015 by The Lockman Foundation, La Habra, CA 90631. All rights reserved.

Scripture marked (MEV) is taken from the Modern English Version. Copyright © 2014 by Military Bible Association. Used by permission. All rights reserved.

Scripture marked (TLB) is taken from The Living Bible copyright © 1971 by Tyndale House Foundation. Used by permission of Tyndale House Publishers Inc., Carol Stream, Illinois 60188. All rights reserved.

Scripture marked (BSB) is taken from The Berean Bible (www.Berean.Bible) Berean Study Bible (BSB) © 2016-2020 by Bible Hub and Berean.Bible. Used by Permission. All rights Reserved.

Scripture marked (ESV) is taken from The ESV® Bible (The Holy Bible, English Standard Version®), copyright © 2001 by Crossway, a publishing ministry of Good News Publishers. Used by permission. All rights reserved.

All rights reserved. No part of this publication may be reproduced or transmitted in any form or by any means, electronic or mechanical, including photocopy, recording, or any information storage retrieval system, without permission in writing from the copyright owner.

For all of God's chosen people who have prayed, cried and walk away this book was written for you to be encouraged. God is yet alive and know the plans he has for his children. I've walked in your shoes and have experienced spiritual struggles and have been ordained to live as a witness for the Kingdom of heaven.
Trust the lord and lean not to your own understanding. Will you accept the challenge today and share your testimony to others?

Father in heaven I thank you for making me a living testimony. You are the love of my life and my strong tower. I know without a doubt this book will transform the lives of each individual who reads it. All the glory belongs to you. In Jesus Name! Amen.

Acknowledgments

To my lord, the God of Abraham, Isaac and Jacob, who have chosen me for such a time as this. I am eternally grateful for your grace and mercy and the loving kindness you continue to display each day.

To all the spiritual mothers who fervently intercede for me & my family.

To the prayer warriors in North Carolina who labor on the prayer line for souls daily.

To my spiritual sisters (Prophetess Gail Dunlap & Pastor Ileana Web) who have been spiritual and mentally instrumental in the Kingdom.

To all six of children (Jlyne, Josira, Jarrod, Nykesseia, Johan and Jeremy) who have accepted God as their savior and support the high calling on my life.

To all of those who have been faithful encouragers through my trials and tribulations.

To Pastor Sheryl & Tim Houska for recognizing the gift of intercession and allowing me to use in the ministry.

To the spiritual leaders and saints who have labored before the mighty lord and prayed for the perfect will of the lord to be done on earth in my life as it is in heaven.

To Jera Publishing (Kimberly Martin) who diligently worked to make this book available worldwide.

To Liberty Baker(Editor) who showed favor and patience in the editorial phase.

Special Thanks

To my mother (Gloria Malone) who have stood by my side faithfully.

To Mother Evelyn Foster who lived an authentic holy life and shared personal experience and great testimonies.

To Mother Audrey Belvedere who is in the bosom of the lord, a bold believer of Christ who displayed the mantle of Anna's anointing daily.

To Sis Melody Sanders in loving memory, a true representation of a proverb 31 woman and my spiritual mother with a sweet spirit who led me to Christ and lived the apostolic doctrine.

Contents

In the Womb! 1
The Teen Meltdown 5
The First Achievement 11
The Club Life 15
Divine Intervention 19
My Spiritual Conversion 21
A New Creature in Christ 29
The Backslider 33
Restoration by the Blood 37
The Painful Trial 43
Overcoming Singleness 53
The Oil of Gladness 59
Discovering My Purpose 67
Walking in my Destiny 73
The Victor 81

In the Womb!

Before I formed you in the womb I knew you, before you were born I set you apart; I appointed you as a prophet to the nations. – Jeremiah 1:5, NIV

Blood pooled on the ground under my mother's leg as she lay on the ground crying and not moving. As a five-year-old girl, I stood on the porch watching and crying. Paramedics jumped out of the truck and began to surround my mother. I continued watching as the paramedics tried to help. When my aunt drove up, she told me and my brother to get into her car while she began asking the paramedics and authorities questions. Eventually, the ambulance drove away with my mother, and my aunt took us to her home.

I grew up in a small friendly community where everyone treated each other like family. Most of the neighbors were senior citizens who had been living on the street for many years. My best friend lived across the street and we would often ride our bikes, play jump rope, and play other outdoor games. My childhood was simple, and I had a good life, but I could never understand why my mother kept her alcoholic boyfriend in her life. The man would drink every Friday on pay day then catch a taxi to our house, and there were many times he would stagger from the taxi and end up face-flat on the ground when he got out. The day my mother was rushed to the hospital her boyfriend had been trying to dance with her when he lost his grip and my mother fell on the ground. He was so drunk that night, and after my mother fell on the ground he ran away.

I grew up in a single parent home with no father. My mother didn't drink or smoke and was kind of a home body. She took care of me and my baby brother and provided comfort, therefore, we didn't really miss having a father figure. As the old saying goes, "How can you miss something you never had?" At the time that my mother had her accident, she was raising her last two children which were me and my younger brother. My brother was four years younger and too young to remember my mother's fall.

When I was a child, we didn't have much and the little we had was provided by the grace of God. I was a happy child and enjoyed playing outside with my friends. We had lots of elderly individuals living in our neighborhood and sometimes they would ask me to run errands for them or clean up their house. One of the neighbors who lived down the street, Ms. Grant, had suffered a stroke, and as a result, one of her arms was paralyzed. She began calling me over to help her wash her hair and clean the house. This taught me that it feels good to help the senior citizens in your community.

I was not raised in a church, however, we had a family-centered Baptist church that my mother would visit on occasion. My mother didn't know how to drive, and we would walk or ride the bus to and from the places we needed to go. Mother was fearless in those days and sometimes we would leave the house during the evening to visit a relative and it would be very dark when we returned home on foot. Me and my brother were petrified by barking of the dogs in the dark, however, we felt secure while walking with my mom.

Every night, mom would play the radio and listen to the gospel station. She would cry and praise the Lord and I would just watch her until I feel asleep. We were not able to attend church much because the church was located outside of the local bus transportation area. I didn't know much about God, but when my mother was in the intensive care unit for over three months as a result of her accident with her drunk boyfriend, we had to live with an older family member, Aunt Kart. She was religious and taught me and my brother how to say a prayer every night. She would also make us read scriptures from the Bible. We had a strict schedule of cleaning the house and washing clothes before we were allowed to play outside.

Our Aunt Kart's strictness meant that she also believed in discipline. I recall one day when I drew on the fridge with a blue marker and then lied about it. Once I finally admitted doing it, she made me go outside and pick three switches. My rear end and legs were bruised for a week! There's nothing like getting a whipping in nothing but undergarments! The house had to stay clean at all times, and after we played with toys, we immediately placed them back in the toy box. The dishes had to be spotless and even at the age of nine, if there were food stains on the pots I would have to wash them over again.

We prayed every night for God to heal our mother so she could get well and take care of us again. Aunt Kart took us to church every Sunday and this is when I was introduced to living as a baptized believer. Living with Aunt Kart opened the door for me to know there was a God.

Finally, our prayers were answered, and my mother recovered from her injuries and the two of us were able to return home to live with her. She had been healed by God, but she would be forever disabled because of the steel rod placed in her to support her hip (just testify). Her disability didn't matter to me, I was just happy to have my mother back home and out of the hospital.

We lived in a one-bedroom apartment which is still standing today, and I can remember my mother receiving government assistance to take care of the two of us. There were times when we had little food in the house but me, my mom, and my brother would walk over to our cousin's house and get food that we stored in their deep freezer.

Soon I was a thirteen-year-old, rapidly maturing teenage girl who wanted her own private space. I really didn't ask for anything from the Lord, however I wanted my own bedroom. Our one-bedroom apartment had a small living room, bedroom, kitchen, and bathroom. Me and my brother slept with our mother even though there was a bed in the living room area and two beds in my mom's bedroom.

One day, I remember kneeling down in the small bathroom and talking with God. This was my first one on one conversation with God and I asked Him if He would give my mother a bigger house so that I could have my own bedroom. One year later the Lord blessed my family with a three-bedroom apartment, and I had my own bedroom. God answered my prayer at thirteen years old (just testify).

Even at the earliest stage of my life, God was there, even though I couldn't see evidence of Him. Sometimes we don't understand our purpose in life, however when the plan of God manifests, we must continue to trust Him. When there is a divine plan, nothing can stop the perfect will of God.

The Teen Meltdown

"For I know the plans I have for you," declares the Lord, "plans to prosper you and not to harm you, plans to give you hope and a future." - Jeremiah 29:11-13, NIV

At the age of sixteen, I lay in the hospital, scared, and crying while giving birth to my firstborn, a healthy baby girl (just testify). Thoughts ran wild in my head as I tried to figure out what happened to my life. I could hear all the voices that were telling me that I would never be anything, I'd be a dropout teen with nothing. My life was messed up now, what would I become?

Let me take you back to how this part of my life began. I was fifteen years old, and I was a very timid, quiet teenager. I would go to school, come home, eat, take a nap, and watch television. Yes, I was a momma's girl who happened to also be a virgin. My mom was an older lady and didn't talk about the birds and the bees at all, and actually, when my period started at the age of fourteen, it may sound crazy, but I was completely unprepared

Just Testify

and I knew nothing about it. I was scared and told my younger brother I was about to die.

Stompford High School was my favorite high school because most of us grew up in the same community, so over half of the students were in elementary school together. But I was the biggest nerd you could ever meet. I could show you my ninth-grade pictures to prove it, with my mouth open wide and wearing the ugliest sweater anyone had ever seen before. I was happy, and I really enjoyed talking with my best friend at school. But I was also one of very few virgins at school.

I joined the band and was on the band flag team. I was very timid and mainly kept to myself. Three of my classmates, all boys, would tease me about being a virgin and because I thought it was disgusting, I would ignore their crude remarks. I didn't like any of those three obnoxious, disgusting boys.

This went on for months, and then one day, one of the boys from my school stopped by my house without my permission and knocked on the door. My sister, Lona, answered the door and yelled out my name to come. Of course, when she said his name, I didn't move from my chair. I was afraid of boys and just didn't want to be around them. My sister, on the other hand, was raised by a family friend and was visiting our family at the time. She was teasing with me and the boy from the school. She told him, "Denise is afraid of boys and she is not coming out of the house." It was all true and I told him no, I didn't want to walk with him. The boy said, "Let's go for a walk. My grandmother lives just around the corner and I am going to visit her. She is at home, I promise. We will be back in minutes."

Again, my response was, "No," and I went back in the house. Lona came inside and said to me, "He's not trying to get in your panties, and you need to get out of the house. What harm will it do you to walk with the boy?

Well, you can guess that after my sister convinced me to take a walk with him, we got to his grandmother's house and she was not at home. He told me to sit on the sofa while he got a drink out the fridge. He came back into the room and sat really close to me and began to try to kiss and touch me. I asked him to stop and move over, but that didn't work. I ended up losing the long fight and lost my virginity that night.

Three months later I was sitting in the classroom feeling sleepy and I dosed off to sleep. I wondered why I felt so tired and sleepy. It was so hard to stay awake and I wasn't sure why. The bell rang for the students to transition to their next class, and I saw the boy who invited me to his grandmother's house that day. He came up to me and asked, "How are you feeling?" Remember, as I said before, I wasn't attracted to this guy nor did I have any affection toward him prior to the night we went on that walk.

Now I couldn't stand him and ignored him and walked to my next class. Two weeks went by, and the boy came up to me again and said, "I made a bet with the other boys, I was going to be the first one to break your virginity and the only way to prove it was to get you pregnant." My mother had no idea I was no longer a virgin, and one day I got sick so my mom took me to the emergency room where they confirmed that I was pregnant. My mother was disappointed and with concern in her voice, she looked at me and said "Denise!"

During my entire pregnancy, I was very depressed, and I really just wanted to quit on life. I would have conversations with God and ask Him why I had to be the one that got pregnant when all those fast hot girls were out there having sex and I was the one who would have no future. I had big plans of becoming successful one day. The statistics of teenage mothers is very high, and the statistics are usually true. The thoughts were in my mind on ways I could just kill myself and end it all.

I didn't have anyone to confess to or talk to about my concerns, and I was not going to tell my mother I had been thinking of giving up on life. Besides, my mother didn't believe in committing suicide and said that if someone did so, "their soul would burn in hell."

When my oldest sister, Mona, who was in the Army, heard the news about me being pregnant, she purchased a greyhound ticket for me to travel to Arizona. When we finally arrived in Arizona, my sister picked me and my younger brother up from the bus station. When we got to her apartment she said, "I have scheduled an appointment with an abortion clinic tomorrow, and if you have the abortion you will be able to finish school." She also said, "If you have this child, you will never be anything and your life will be ruined forever." Now, I guess you can figure out this is the last thing I needed to hear due to the depression I had been feeling and I was being forced to make a decision to abort my unborn child. Wow, this really was a shock too, because my mother was against having abortions, so basically, my sister tricked my mother into allowing the two of us to travel to Tucson when all along, my sister had her own intentions.

The next day, we drove to the Family Intervention clinic and my sister signed the papers saying that she was my legal mother without even asking me if I wanted to go through with this procedure. She bribed me and said, "I will pay you $500 dollars and will take you shopping after you recover in two days." Here we go again. My mind was running wild with thoughts of what my mother would say about this. How would God see this? Was this the right thing to do? I was fifteen years old with all of these questions and a big decision to make in a very short amount of time.

After my sister left, I begin to talk to God with tears rolling down my face, asking Him for directions and answers. Then I asked the office staff if I could make a call to my mother in Georgia. They said, "Your mother just left." I told them that my mother lives in Georgia and the person who filled out the application was my oldest sister.

I did make the call to Georgia and spoke to a family member and left a message for my mom. The clinical staff refused the procedure because my legal parent must complete the paperwork, so I called my sister and explained, and as you can imagine, she was very upset and began to say very damaging things to me, such as, "You will never be anything after this baby is born," and "I hope this baby bursts your tail open." I was crying, scared, and hopeless because I didn't follow through on the abortion that my sister thought I should have.

After travelling to Arizona, I did receive a revelation from the Lord and this brings me forward to when I was in the labor and delivery room, giving birth to my baby. I heard, "Give us one big push. It's a girl!"

For the young teenager reading this book, be encouraged, my dear. You are a winner, and the Lord does not make mistakes. You and your baby have a purpose, and this does not mean your life is over. Trust God and believe there is a reason and it will all "work together for good" (Romans 8:28, NKJV).

The First Achievement

I can do all things through him who strengthens me. – Philippians 4:13, NASB

I received a phone call while at school one day and the neighbor on the other end of the line said that my two-year-old baby was found walking around alone. I ran as fast as I could to get home from school to find out why my two-year-old baby were wandering the neighborhood alone, wearing only a t-shirt and a diaper? I could only recall this moment with dread, and all I could think about was my little girl's protection and finding a safe environment so I could continue my education. My heart dropped when I received that call, and I knew I had to make a big decision. "This is it for me, and now I have to quit school to take care of my child," I thought. I was in the eleventh grade at the time and I was so close to getting my diploma.

The word spread through the family that the mother of my baby's father was a social worker with the Department of Family

Just Testify

& Children Services. She said to me, "You are not going to quit school," and told me to complete the application for childcare assistance. This was a process that could take weeks before any services could be rendered. I stopped by a local daycare in my neighborhood and asked the owner how much childcare would cost for a two-year-old. I didn't have a job and I had no money except for the $200 hundred dollar assistance money from the government. The owner, Dr. Nottle, was a graduate and professor from Albany State University and she owned several businesses in the community. She told me to bring my daughter to the daycare while I wait for assistance and she would care for the baby without pay. I could see the favor of the Lord on my life when this need was provided. The childcare assistance was approved, my baby was placed in a safe learning environment, and I could stay in school.

God will assign the right individuals to motivate you to achieve the next level of growth in your life. It was the day of graduation, and I had made it through many tough times which could only testify to God's presence in my life once again.(just testify) My classmates were all planning to party the night after graduation and everyone was talking about getting drunk and having fun. Drinking alcohol was not my thing, however there were a few occasions when I was younger that I would taste my mom's boyfriend's wine cooler in the fridge. As a young teenager on the day of my graduation, I remember thinking, "I've never been drunk before, so at the party, maybe I can see what it feels like." The graduation took place and we received our diplomas.

Later that evening, my head started to hurt really bad and I took pain medication, but it was still hurting very bad. This was the first time I had ever had a migraine and it was unbearable. The paramedics were called and they took me and my mother to the hospital. As I sat in the emergency waiting room feeling like my head was spinning, I thought in my mind, "What is wrong with me?" We sat, waiting to be seen, for more than six hours, and in the meantime, my headache worsened. It hurt so bad I couldn't cry anymore but my mom was trying to comfort me.

Finally, we were called into the back to see the doctor and he ordered blood work and a cat scan. We spent the entire night at the hospital waiting for the results from the blood work and then the doctor came in the room and said it was a migraine and gave me a shot for pain. The nurse provided me with a referral to a neurologist for follow-up. When I saw the neurologist, they ordered more tests and told me that it was all sinus related. And can I just testify here that I truly believe in my heart that it was not meant for me to party and get drunk with my classmates, and the Lord intervened that night.

I wanted to be finished with school and I didn't plan to pursue college, however, Dr. Nottle, my role model and mentor, decided to give me an application package to attend Albany State University, her alumni. However, at the time, I declined to complete the application and found a job working as a cashier at the local Krystal restaurant.

My first job gave me the ability to live independently and to qualify for a low-income apartment where my daughter and I could live together. I was very happy to be free from high school and now I could live my life my own way. Now I was working the graveyard shift at the Krystal as a cashier on the weekends. The crowds were rowdy with crazy people who were leaving the night clubs and the only place to get fast food was at Krystal's. There were a lot of creepy characters, drunk women, men, homeless people, and the devoted club goers. At this stage in my life, I was not sure about my future such as a career, goals, and an education. I didn't want to attend a four-year college, and in my mind, I just didn't see further education as an option that I wanted.

One flashback of my time at the Krystal was when Jessie Mae, a grill cooker at the restaurant, was sharing her life story about all the years she had been working at Krystal. She said, "I am stuck at this place and this was not my plan." I was listening and watching her teach me how to cook the Krystal burgers. I noticed her wrinkled hands, and something popped into my brain. I thought, "I don't want to be stuck working at this place for the rest of my life and I need to make a decision to prepare for my future." All I could think about was taking care of my two-year-old daughter and making sure I had the means to support her in every way.

Yes, I finally made my decision to go back to school and I enrolled at Albany Technical College and chose Office Technology Management as my major. I was determined not to attend a four-year college program. But a good man's steps are ordered by God and there are individuals who are divinely positioned in our lives to lead us to our destiny. Always remember it's not your plan, but our heavenly Father's plans that matter. Surrendering to God's plan is a step toward spiritual growth. Let go and let God!

The Club Life

He who covers his sins shall not prosper, but whoso confesseth and forsaketh them shall have mercy. – Proverbs 28:13, KJV

*E*verybody dance now! Give me the music playing in the background while we are grooving to the beat. I'm at the club on the dance floor with my girl and we are having fun. This was the weekends for us. We would go out to the E-Club and party. Celebrating for graduating from Albany Technical College with a diploma in Office management (just testify). Although we enjoyed going out on a Saturday night, there was no drinking alcohol or getting drunk, we hung out to mix and mingle. I was working at the restaurant at night and attending college during the day. One night, on the military base at the club, I meet this man (a jar head) and we exchanged numbers.

Cupid had struck me, or so I thought, the guy from the club called and we met for dinner a few times. Three months later, he called and said, "I want to be more than friends." To make a long story short, we began to date and then moved in together, or to clarify, he moved in with me. We were in a committed relationship and it was official. The two of us, along with my two children, were one big family. However, the elderly women in the neighborhood would ask me almost every week, "Honey, are you still shacking?" This phrase would send chills through my warm body and I could not shake the guilty feeling of living in sin.

Living as a Baptist believer, I knew fornication was a sin and this was indicated in the Holy Bible. We were Baptist's and back then people willfully sinned and would continue to live a normal life. It would puzzle my mind to think we could continue to sin over and over again and God would forgive us each time. Each time I would fornicate there was a conviction that would come over my body. I would kneel on my knees and pray, "Lord please forgive me for sinning. Lord, there are so many religions out there, how do I know which one is the right one?" The Holy Bible was a familiar book you would find laying open on the coffee table in the living room as I was growing up, but I can't remember reading the Bible. As a little girl, I was taught to say the Lord's prayer every night before bed. When I said it, it would sound like this "Our father who are in heaven, hollowed would be thy name. Thy kingdom come and thy will be done, on earth as it is in heaven. Forgive us this day as we forgive out debtors, lead us not into temptation but deliver us from sin, and if I die before I wake, I pray to God my soul be saved." Young kids will always leave out a word or two, but you get the point.

I continued to live in fornication, go out to the clubs, attend school, care for my children, and "play house" as my mother would call it. Riding in the car with my Robert one day, I cried out loud in pain. As I held my stomach, the pain was unbearable. My boyfriend drove me to the emergency room, and the doctor ordered bloodwork and a urine sample. I was released and told that it was just a bladder infection. Months go by and everything was good with my life. My man with perfect credit pays all my bills and buys a car for cash. I got to spend money on clothes and shoes for me and the kids. Robert was a great financial steward and he paid my tuition and I had my needs supplied.

When Robert moved in with me, it was a surprise to me that he was a working alcoholic. Yes, I know, military guys do drink and party and his thing was partying on the weekends. Of course, ladies, in my mind I was thinking that yes, we met at the club, but we decided to settle down and play house, so we should not hang out at the club on the weekends anymore. It was all wrong in my mind, the dude continued to party hard at the club and get drunk. And about this time, I gave birth to our son, and I was grateful that he was a healthy baby boy.(just testify)

I was no longer happy at this point and I getting angry. Something had to change. He was still partying, and I had stopped clubbing thinking that we were going to make this relationship work. We had a talk and I asked him to stop going to the clubs and stay home and spend time with the family. He didn't agree to do what I asked so we argued all the time and I gave him a demand. I told him, "Either you stop going to clubs and we go out together, or I will start back going to the club." Guess what, he didn't stop, and I went back to the club life on Saturday nights.

Divine Intervention

But God proves his love for us in that while we still were sinners Christ died for us. - Romans 5:8, NRSV

Everything in my life was spinning out of control and going downhill very fast. I was living in sin by having an ungodly relationship, and it's safe to say, Amen, somebody! I was unequally yoked, creating soul ties, and being influenced by the strongman all at once. Robert and I were cheating on each other and clubbing on the weekends. He would stalk me and my friend trying to find out what I was doing. He would stay out all night and come home the next day and then we would get into arguments. I was trying to end the ungodly relationship, but he refused to leave.

Ouch! The severe pain in my stomach returned and now it was more intense. I went to the doctor who kept telling me that it's just a bladder infection. I had been taking antibiotics for a week now and the pain was still there. By now I couldn't even walk because it hurt so bad. The pain medication wasn't working, and the heating pad didn't make me feel any better. Robert took me to the hospital and left. I was in the room by myself while the doctor ran more medical tests.

Tears began to roll down my face as I lay in the hospital bed with excruciating pain, wondering if I was going to die. I began to talk to God saying, "God, if you are real, please let the doctors find out what is wrong with me. I am sorry for all my sin and I need you now." Two hours passed, then three, then finally the E.R. doctor came into my room and said, "We found the problem and we have good and bad news. The good news is that you have an ovarian cyst on your right ovary the size of a large grapefruit and its non-cancerous. The bad news is that it has twisted and damaged your right fallopian tube which has ruptured. We have to do emergency surgery in the morning, and we will have to perform a partial hysterectomy due to the severe damage done to the tube. I was alone with no cell phone and no family around to talk to, but God was my comforter.

When I woke up from surgery, I was glad to be alive but I was still in pain. The doctor was standing over my bed saying to me, "The surgery went well. We removed the cyst but left both your ovaries and the fallopian tube." Another testimony of God's goodness! A twenty-two-year-old told by the doctor you must have a partial hysterectomy, but God, Saints! Proverbs 3:5-6 (Version) says,(just testify) "Trust in the lord with all your heart and lean not on your own understanding. In all your ways acknowledge him and he shall direct your paths."

God does answer a sinner's prayer. There are many times that we are living in sin throughout our lives, and many Believers make it seem as though God does not care about those who consistently sin; however, I beg to differ. God loves everyone. The Word says in John 3:16 (NKJV), "For God so loved the world that He gave His only begotten Son, that whoever believes in Him should not perish but have everlasting life.

My Spiritual Conversion

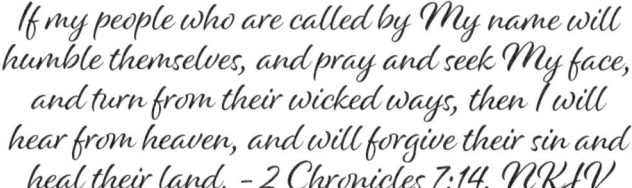

If my people who are called by My name will humble themselves, and pray and seek My face, and turn from their wicked ways, then I will hear from heaven, and will forgive their sin and heal their land. - 2 Chronicles 7:14, NKJV

As I lay on the table in the doctor's office, clenching the table and trying not to scream, the doctor snatched staples from my lower stomach area. "Your body is healing well," the doctor says as I think how grateful I am for the evidence of the Holy Spirit's healing power in my life. Soon everything was back to normal. I was still living in sin with Robert and there was no peace in the house. The day came that I had another graduation and I received my A.S. Business degree, and, another testimony of God's presence in my life, I was set to find a good paying job. (just testify)

Robert was not happy about my graduation because he was afraid I was going to leave him now. He would say manipulative things to me, such as, "You have more kids now, you will never make it without me." Mental abuse is serious and we must understand it can bring down our self-esteem. Being unequally yoked and spiritually disconnected will create a dysfunctional lifestyle.

I started tossing and turning all night, sweating in my dreams, and feeling like I was being attacked. By what or who, I wasn't sure. There was no physical body standing over me, but I was fearful to close my eyes. Something was trying to take my breath away; it would feel like I was suffocating. I began to think I was losing my mind and I didn't feel like I could share this with anyone. I wondered if maybe I needed to visit a mental health facility. This was the first time I had experienced this, and I needed help, but I didn't know what to do.

Two weeks passed and I began to have demonic dreams constantly. I began to lose sleep because I was afraid to sleep. I was thinking in my head that something was trying to kill me. I would lay in the bed and feel like my body was paralyzed, but it seemed that I was awake even though I couldn't move my body or make my voice scream. All I could feel was a strong presence that would not let me sleep. It was tormenting me in my sleep until I would finally wake up. I began to feel depressed about the nightmares I had been having for months now. For some reason, I began to think it was time for me to die. I remember thinking, "Why do I feel like something is trying to take my life?" I was too ashamed to talk with anyone about this. I thought they would think I was crazy, and I began to think that maybe I was crazy.

If something like this is happening in your life, here is a spiritual warfare prayer that I would like to pray over you right now: "I bind every demonic attack and loose the anointing of the Lord onto your life. The blood of Jesus protects you and your family. You shall live and not die."

If you are and have been experiencing spiritual attacks in your sleep, anoint your body, and everything and everyone in your house. Read Psalm 91 aloud while walking around your house every day. Recite Psalm 91 aloud in your car before you drive off to work and teach your children, grandchildren, nieces, and nephews to memorize Psalm 91 and to say it each day.

"The thief comes only in order to steal and kill and destroy. I came that they may have and enjoy life, and have it in abundance [to the full, till it overflows]" (John 10:10, AMP). Don't open up your house to evil spirits but continue to cast out demons and demonic forces by speaking the Word of God. I anoint my house, the windows, the doors, my children's shoes, their beds, their pillows, and everything I can think of. Remember, your children are watching everything you say and do around them.

When my kids were younger, before I began praying to God, I would tell my children, "Mom needs to ask God to pay the rent." I would then go into my room and close the door and pray. My children knew what I was doing and when the rent was paid, I would ask them, "Who did this for us?" Their response was, "Jesus."

My children are adults now and whenever they find themselves in trouble, they call and say, "Mom, let's pray." Each one of them know how to pray to God because when they were younger, they watched me praying. Each one of them carries anointing oil with them daily and recites Psalm 91 to summon the angels of heaven to keep them protected. Are they perfect? No, they are not, but we must use wisdom to train our children to know the mighty Lord we serve and to know His surpassing love.

At my doctor's office, I was waiting to be called into the back to see the physician. A nice young lady sat next to me. She smiled at me and began to talk to me, and we conversed until the nurse's aid called my name to go back in the room to be seen by the doctor. The nice lady's name was Sis Thomas. She gave me her number and I gave her mine, and later in the same month Sis Thomas called and we talked over the phone. She began to tell me that God is a Savior and He died so that we could have life. She shared her testimonies of how God saved and filled her with the Holy Spirit. I felt good when I talked with her, however, she made me nervous. I would get afraid when she would tell me about being filled with the Holy Spirit. What is the Holy Spirit? I had never heard this before. Sis Thomas invited me to attend church services, so I accepted the offer.

Sis Thomas and her husband, Bernie Thomas, who is a minister for God, stopped by the house and they met my kids. We talked and laughed for hours and it was fun listening as they shared their love story.

"Wake up, everyone! Eat breakfast! We are going to church!" I shouted out in my house to my kids. This is the very first time I can recall taking my children to a local church. Everyone got dressed, we hopped in the car to ride off to church. My nerves were racing as I walked into the church doors holding my young son's hand. The church people seemed to be friendly and it was an apostolic church, whatever that meant, I had no idea at the time. The choir sang and I noticed that all the women had a covering on top of their heads. I wasn't sure what it was, but I would continue to enjoy the Sunday service.

Months pass and the kids and I continued attending church services. Sis Thomas and I became good friends and I learn that she has a sweet spirit. Have you ever met someone with a sweet spirit? Whenever she was around me, she was loving, kind, and peaceful. She had a low toned voice and a small built body frame. She would close her eyes and worship the Lord and tell me that closing your eyes helps to block out distractions. It helps you to put your mind on Jesus and concentrate on things that are pure and holy.

I enjoyed church services, however the members danced and praised God almost the entire service. Everyone praised God in the spirit, and when the praise team sang, the people would begin to dance and even the little babies would shout. I had never experienced church services like this before. The pastor would shout and jump on the floor and in the chairs. The members would praise God for the entire service. I thought, "Lord, do these people ever get tired of shouting?" The pastor invited new visitors to join after he preached, and I stood up with my kids and walked to the altar. What a relief it was knowing that I was now a member of local church.

The church had tarrying services on Thursday nights, and I wasn't sure what that meant, but I would soon find out. The pastor began to teach from the Scripture passage in Acts 2:38 (Version), "Peter spoke to the crowd, repent change your old way of thinking, turn from your sinful ways, and be baptized in the name of Jesus and you will receive the gift of the holy spirit."

After attending church and new member classes, I decided to show up for Thursday night tarrying services. As I am walking down to the altar, I see other members on their knees crying out, "Jesus, Jesus, Jesus." There were leaders who were comforting others who are on their knees saying, "That's it, call him by his name, let him work on you. Tell God you repent and you are godly-sorry for all your sins."

Soon it's my turn and my nerves were all over the place. I began to call on the name of Jesus as tears rolled down my face. I felt this presence, I'm not sure what it was, but it's hard to explain it. I was very scared and not sure what to do with this feeling, so I stood up and told Sis Thomas I was ready to go home. She hugged me and gave me comfort and said, "It's going to be alright."

The next day, Sis Thomas and I had a conversation about tarrying for the Holy Spirit. She says, "Sis Jackie, it's the spirit of God that He promises to give as a gift and the Holy Spirit will teach us how to live holy and victorious lives. There is no fear in Jesus, but we have to trust Him. Do you trust His Word? Remember, the Bible tells us that God loved the world so much that he gave his only begotten son so we can have everlasting life. (John 3:16, MEV). I decided to attend the next tarrying services and this time I stayed on the altar until the Holy Spirit filled my mouth and I began to speak in tongues. It was like a slow type of speech at first with lots of drooling and crying. One of the members said, "She's got it!" This was the most nervous and exciting day of my life (just testify).

There were teachings 2 Corinthians 5:17 on being a new creature in Christ and about how old things are passed away and new things have come. I was now saved and satisfied, but Robert and I were still living together. Robert and I had to talk, and when we did, I told him that I had been filled with the Holy Spirit and fornication is a sin. I told him we could no longer participate in sin. He was frustrated and said, "I don't believe in your God, there is no God." He didn't like the fact that my life of fornication was over and now I was a new creature in Christ. I told him he would have to move out, because we are not married and can't continue to shack. He refused to leave and said to me, "I am not going anywhere, and I will kill you before I let you leave me."

I kept going to church and the other Saints and I prayed for God to move in my situation. The mother of the church said to me, "Is there anything too hard for God?" Two months had passed and one night after Bible study, the kids and I went home and found Robert packing his car with his clothes. He didn't say anything, he just kept taking boxes of his clothes to his car. Finally, after the last box he said, "I am gone."

My Spiritual Conversion

Remember that salvation is free and we must understand that the Word tells us to present our bodies a living sacrifice, holy and acceptable unto God. You may be crying out to God and asking, "Why Lord?" But trust God to move in your situation. It's our Lord's desire to fill all His children with His spirit. Turn away from sin, my sister, my brother, don't look back, but run from sin and cry out to our Father in heaven and watch your life change for the greater.

A New Creature in Christ

Therefore if any man be in Christ, he is a new creature: old things are passed away; behold, all things are become new. - 2 Corinthians 5:17, KJV

"Praise the Lord, everybody, praise the Lord! Clap your hands, everybody better clap your hands," is the song the choir sang at the start of the church service. Attending church service three days a week, not including revivals, I was no longer wearing pants, nor was my daughter. I went out and purchased different colored head coverings for women. I wore my dresses and skirts below my knees and sometimes to my ankles. My friend circle had changed and now my focus was on serving God, working, taking care of my children, and attending church three days a week. Living holy means, no more fornication, lying, and doing things against the Word of God. No dancing to music all night long, and no staying up late at night on the phone with a male friend. My conversations had changed for the better.

My new relationship with God had started and I had devoted my time and energy to seeking God's purpose for my life.

I was a full-time student and a full-time employee and taking care of my children as a single mother. The Thomases were now my spiritual parents and we became part of one big spiritual family. The Saints would fellowship at church while my children would play with other kids at the church. Every 3rd Sunday, the church served a free dinner for members and guests. We all worked together in unity to build the Kingdom of God. My pastor would preach on holy living by obeying God's Word. And he would teach us that the Word stated that the Saints should meditate on the Word of God day and night.

I began learning about God and His Holy Spirit each day. I became baptized by water in the name of Jesus and began speaking in tongues. Yes, I am a believer, however it does not mean my life was perfect. I found out that the devil was not happy with my new walk with God when Robert began sending me threatening letters saying that he wanted the car he purchased for me. It had been over two years now, and he repeatedly sent messages by cousins that it was "his car." Struggling to make ends meet, I was working full-time, but my paycheck was very little. The government assistance did help with putting food on the table. Family members were telling me I was crazy to give up wearing pants and told me I was living like a nun. They said it was crazy to make my children go to church all those nights. Old friends began asking me, "Why are you doing all this? Is it worth doing all this?"

My response was, "Why not give up these things? Jesus gave His life and hung on the cross for us. Why not give up wearing pants and stop sinning so I can go to heaven one day? I don't want to burn in hell for eternity and I have to obey His Word."

As a new baby in Christ, I found myself feeling lonely and a bit confused, and not really understanding the Word of God when I read it. Praying in the Holy Spirit did help to stay focused and to continue to trust God. There were many nights that I would cry, not knowing how a bill would get paid or where the gas money would come from. The devil would whisper in my ear night and day, "When you were with Robert, you didn't have to struggle. He paid all your bills and took care of you and the kids." I began praying harder than ever now, asking God to make a way for my family.

Robert stopped by my mom's house and told my mom that he still loved me and if I were to take him back he would buy anything I needed, including a brand new car. I began dealing with temptation in my flesh, but I hid the Word in my heart. This helped me to resist the devil so that he would flee. I am grateful to be saved and filled with the Holy Spirit because there are many people who are not saved and have died not knowing the true gospel of Jesus.

The mother of the church had been saved for many years. She instructed me to write a letter to God with my prayer request. The Scripture tells us in Matthew 7:7 (Version), "Ask and it shall be given, seek and you shall find, knock and the door shall be open." My prayer requests were written in the letter and here is a sneak peek of the request, "God bless me with a saved, sanctified, and loving husband, filled with the Holy Spirit. A husband who loves you with all of his heart. I need a good job with better benefits and more pay. Bless me, Lord, with my own brand-new car and a bigger house for my kids and I to live comfortably. Robert keeps sending word messages requesting for the car he purchased for me during the time we were shacking."

Me and my family went to a dealership to look at cars one day when the salesman came out and introduced himself. He escorted us into the office and gave me an application to fill out. Once I completed the application, we headed out to look at the cars on the lot. I was nervous that I would be turned down by the banks because I never made a major purchase like this before. I took several cars out for a test drive and finally decided on a red four-door sedan. It was a stick shift which I knew how to drive because my ex-boyfriend, Robert, had a sports car and he would teach different techniques on driving a stick shift.

So this was a good purchase for me. The salesman told me that manual-shift cars save gas for the buyers, and all I needed now was $500 for a down payment. At the time, I didn't have the money for the payment, however the salesman said to just bring the five hundred dollars back in two weeks. Praise the Lord, God answered my prayers and, as another testimony to God's hand in my life, I was driving my new red Chevy Malibu off the car lot.

Now when Robert found out about the new car, he was shocked and puzzled because he didn't believe my prayers would be answered by the Lord. The prayers of the righteousness availed much, and two weeks later, the Lord touched Robert's heart and he signed the old car title into my name and I sold the car for $500 (just testify).

The Backslider

Come back to me, my wayward sons, says the Lord, for I am your true master. I'll take you, one from a city and two from a family, and bring you back to Zion. - Jeremiah 3:14, Version

Water was everywhere. Emergency sirens could be heard throughout the neighborhoods. We had to grab anything we could, but we were left with no choice but leave our home. Children were crying and water was flooding into the homes on the streets. Some didn't make it out in time, and dead bodies could be seen floating in the street. Large and small buildings were covered in water. Thank God my family survived the Flint River flooding.

The next question in our minds was how the flood had affected our church. We learned that it was damaged by the flood and now the Saints were scattered everywhere. We wondered where the members would have Bible study or morning worship service. The city was devastated by the natural disaster and many now didn't have homes or cars. Shelters were opened and packed with hungry people and children. The rooftops of homes and buildings were covered by muddy, dirty water. The Believers scattered, and some began to have church services in their homes. The little apostolic church was washed away in the flood, and the pastor and his wife decided to relocate to Florida.

Prior to the flood, the pastor warned the Saints to show love and walk in the fruits of the Spirit during Sunday services. The news of the pastor relocating was spreading like a contagious virus and the members were quarreling with one another. In the book of Timothy, he discusses the Saints should not be in conflict against one another but should worship in unity. Our congregation was small, and it appeared to represent the fruits of the Spirit prior to joining the ministry. We know the enemy will use any vessel available, especially those who are not walking in the Spirit of the Lord.

Serving God had become the center of my life and I was really enjoying praising the Lord. Yet, still a baby in Christ, there was much to learn from reading and meditating on God's Word. Living holy is not easy and it's not hard, it's the way of life that Jesus ordained. Apostolic ministry may seem to be a strict way of living for many Believers, however it took time for me and my kids to adjust. The Bible lessons provided guidance on how the Saints should live, what we should say, and how we should conduct ourselves. Over half of the Believers were raised from birth under the Apostolic doctrine and were accustomed to living a consecrated lifestyle.

The women were not allowed to trim or cut their hair and must wear a head covering. When the pastor was praying, there was absolutely no walking because he considered it a disrespect to the Holy Spirit. Altar call was a serious thing, and if a saint was at the altar being delivered, everyone was required to pray in the Spirit. What is a consecrated lifestyle you ask? It means to totally dedicate your life to God by meditating on the Word, fasting, and submitting your body to the Holy Spirit.

1 Peter 2:2 (Version) says, "Like newborn babies, you must crave pure spiritual milk so that you will grow into a full experience of salvation. Cry out for this nourishment and allow the Spirit of the Lord to lead you to the right path." I have been disobedient throughout my spiritual journey, however, I didn't throw in the towel. I just kept praying for strength. There will always be church folks who will try to wedge dissention among the Saints, and this is why Jesus warned the Believers to watch, pray, and stay alert at all times. We all can agree at some point in life there are going to be individuals who rebel in the house of the Lord.

The members in the church were arguing with each other and the disharmony got much worse. There was so much dissention that it led to physical and verbal fights during this time. Listen, I was still a baby in Christ when this was happening, and my mind was baffled to understand why Christian folks would carry on this way. Soon after the flood, I began to backslide into the world and you may ask, "What does it means to backslide?" My interpretation of backsliding is slipping from under the protection of an assigned shepherd and going back into the world. There have been many debates by those who disagree and would say that backsliders are some of us sitting in the ministry at this present time.

I had no desire to go back to clubbing, however I started dating and fornicating again. My kids and I had no spiritual covering, so we stayed home on Sundays and there was no Bible study. The fighting among the church members caused a church split, and I became even more confused. While the local authorities made plans to revitalize the community, the church members were divided and alone. Albany State College campus was under water also which meant no classes for me. I couldn't work, there was no church, and no school, so what was there for me to do?

Two years passed as the community worked to rebuild itself. Now I was working but still had no church to attend. Still a young Christian, I became discouraged with no spiritual directions. Eventually I carried on with attending college, working full-time, and taking care of my kids. A handsome, attractive young male student on campus walked up to me one day while I was sitting in the classroom desk. We shared phone numbers and went out for dinner, and yes, I fell back into fornication again.

When the enemy can keep you from the fellowship of the Saints, you become vulnerable. Your salvation is at risk and there is a trap set by the devil. It's critical to have a church covering and a shepherd to protect your soul. If you don't have a church home, whatever the reason may be, pray and seek God to send you to a God fearing, doctrinally sound ministry. We are overcomers, and the hard times will pass. Be encouraged and believe that the race is not given to the swift nor the strong but to those who will endure to the end. Regardless of what you see with your eyes, trust the Lord because "What is seen is temporary and what is not seen is eternal (2 Corinthians 4:18b, NLT)."

Restoration by the Blood

And I will restore to you years that the locust hath eaten, the cankerworm, and the caterpillar, and the palmerworm, my great army which I sent among you. - Joel 2:25, KJV

I was on my way to hell, my soul was at stake, and this song comes ringing in my ears, "Will you be ready when Jesus comes?" I had been living a celebratory and holy life since I became saved and filled with the Holy Spirit years before. The church spilt had a big impact on my spiritual life. In my mind I was thinking, I had given up wearing pants, given up my sin, and was attending church. Maybe it was not necessary for me to give up all these things. Besides, the members of the church weren't acting like Christians but like fools. Why would God allow the church to split? There are so many questions I didn't have an answer for, so I just decided to continue to live my life my way.

A friend invited me to visit Old Jerusalem Pentecostal church and I accepted. I visited the church with my kids and the pastor and members were very nice. The pastor shared his testimony the Sunday I visited, and he truly was a walking, living miracle, as the church mothers would say. The people praised God but not quite the same as my last church. This church believed in Jesus and the Holy Spirit and I enjoyed visiting. Often, I would walk to the altar and get prayer from the church mother and she begin to speak in my ear, "Lord give her a prayer life, put a prayer life in her, Holy Spirit." Of course, as you can guess, my kids and I soon joined this church.

I rededicated my life to God and began meditating on His Word. This means I had to give up the fornications and turn away from my sins. My children were young, and they adjusted easily to the new church services. Our church had a food pantry as an outreach program that was located next door to the church. My pastor was a very anointed man of God and he would share his vision and dreams about building new affordable homes and making sure the homes were available for those with low-income. The first lady, as we called our pastor's wife, was a sweetheart and we both shared ideas and encouraged each other. Our preacher had such a humble spirit and would cry while sharing his vision with the members. The outreach ministry team consisted of nice people who had a heart for the souls of God's people, and I would volunteer at the outreach center at least two days a week.

Going back to the handsome young man I met on campus, we switched phone numbers and during this transition time into the new church, our relationship was still pretty new. Joe was younger than me, and we began to talk on the phone and go out to dinner and our relationship really moved fast. I was sitting in church hearing the Word of God being preached each Sunday, however I didn't really study God's Word often. The Bible was complicated and when I began to read it, I would think, "What is this passage saying?" There were many moments when I would get agitated with trying to understand and meditate on the Word. Saints, we can't get frustrated because of lack of knowledge. We must develop an intimate relationship with God to allow the Holy Spirit to touch our minds to be able to grasp the meaning of the Scriptures. I was trying to live a single life without fornicating, however once Joe and I connected, my focus was lost. He was all I could think about, and we were together all the time. It was Joe, me, and the kids hanging out together at the local park, the shopping mall, and the ballpark.

Yes, friends, Joe and I were sexually intimate, and wow, we had an amazing relationship. I had never felt this way about any man on this earth and I thought that it must be love. I truly believed I had found my soul mate. Joe finished school and flew back to New York, so we started a long-distance relationship. We would talk on the phone day and night and confess our love for each other. I traveled to New York to meet his family and they were very nice people who embraced me and my kids.

Although, I was happy to be in a church and living for God, the Holy Spirit would not let me rest. The feeling of guilt was over me and I knew God was not happy with my unholy relationship. My spirit man was uneasy, and one day during the church service, the pastor was preaching and he said, "God is looking for holiness and without such, no man shall see God. Is he worth giving up your salvation and spending eternity in hell? If he really loves you, he will marry you." I felt like melting butter after the pastor preached and tears ran freely down my face. My heart was hurting as I sat in church hearing the Word of God but knowing I was not obeying Him.

I felt awful when I realized that even though I loved Joe, He was not worth my salvation. Have you ever felt guilty about willingly participating in something you know the Lord spoke against? For those who have a high calling on your life, you can relate. Later that night, I talked with Joe on the phone and I told him that we had to end our relationship because I couldn't risk losing my soul for him, and besides, I truly loved the Lord with all my heart.

Joe said, "Let's get married and live as a family." When I thought about the choice between hell or marriage, I agreed to marry. 2 Corinthians 6:14 (ASV) says, "Be not unequally yoked together with unbelievers for what fellowship hath righteousness with the unrighteousness?" Well, I didn't ask God if it was His will for me to marry Joe, and I was afraid my Lord would not approve. A sister shared with me how she met her unsaved husband in her backslidden days and they got married and now were both living for God. So I made up my mind that if God could do it for that sister, He could do it for me.

Yes sir, we got married and I felt good knowing that I was no longer fornicating with Joe for he was my husband and God honors marriage.

"ASU!" was the shout you could hear from the seniors at Albany State University, class of 1998. I received my BA from Albany State College in Sociology (just testify).

Our family attended Sunday services faithfully, however, Joe was raised in Catholic church but was no longer a practicing Catholic and was not familiar with holy living and receiving the gift of the Holy Spirit. There were Sundays that Joe could not attend because his job required him to travel out of state. Our first son was born, and we named him a junior after his dad. When Junior was only 8 months old, I conceived me and Joe's first baby girl. We had truly been fruitful and multiplied the land.

The struggles came and our marriage became a rocky roller coaster. Joe was working in another state and I was trying to care of the kids and work a full-time job. I was a Social Worker at the Department of Family & Children Services and the salary was low. Joe made more money than I did but he was working two hours away and only came home on some weekends, but he did send me his checks to pay the bills. This is not how I envisioned my life would be, but I continued to trust God.

Joe and I had a talk about him not attending church for many months. I knew he had to work to provide for the family, but I wanted our family to be together. So I made the suggestion to relocate to Atlanta, Georgia so we could have jobs in the same place and attend church as a family.

One day after making this move to Georgia, Joe shared with me that he didn't have time to attend church and that he didn't see why he should go anyway. He didn't understand the Word and he felt like he was just wasting his time. Keep in mind that English was Joe's second language and this barrier was very challenging for him. But an unequally yoked marriage is not ordained by God and when we go against the will of our Father there are going to be testing times.

I confided in my pastor's wife, who was my spiritual mentor at this time, and she encouraged me to pray for God to save my husband and not give up on him. The instruction I was given may sound easy, however the longsuffering that is required to receive an answer is patiently enduring hardship without complaining of the agony and disappointment. We can all testify of praying for something and feeling like our prayers were not being answered or God was not hearing us. I prayed, prayed, and prayed again for my husband's salvation and for him to be filled with the Holy Spirit. In the meantime, my patience was running out and we were constantly arguing because he refused to attend church.

1 Peter 3:1 (NIV, emphasis added) says, "Wives, in the same way SUBMIT yourselves to your own husbands so that, if any

of them do not believe the word, they may be won over without words by the behavior of their wives." Submission seems to be challenging for those who are accustomed to being in charge and calling the shots prior to marriage. Even my walk with the Lord has been testing at times when it comes to submission, because my spirit man was willing, but the flesh was stubborn. First, we must learn to submit to our Savior's will and refuse to please the flesh. Throughout the Bible, we find that many of God's chosen disciples struggle to submit to the will of the Almighty. Man versus God is not a match, and we must learn to let the Holy Spirit reign in our lives.

Matthew 6:33 (Version) says, "But seek first the kingdom of God and his righteousness and all things will be added to us." For all the single ladies, remember this acrostic: P.U.S.H.—Pray Until Something Happens. Don't get married until you hear a clear "Yes" from the Lord. Don't leave the church until you hear from God, don't make any irrational decision prior to seeking, praying, and fasting while waiting to hear back from God.

Satan hears our prayers too, so know the voice of God and don't allow the enemy to blind you with the spirit of deceptions. Meditate on the Word of God and study the prayer warriors in the Holy Bible. Allow them to serve as examples what authentic prayer sounds like. Paul, Abraham, Moses, and Elijah to list a few men of God who knew how to effectively pray and war in the sprit realm. Spend time with God in your secret closet and allow the Holy Spirit to minister and teach you how to live a victorious life.

The Painful Trial

Count it all joy, my brothers, when you meet trials of various kinds. - James 1:2, Version

A knock came at the door and I opened it to find that it was the police department responding to my call after having a conversation with my teenage daughter. She confessed that Joe had been touching her in appropriately. My belly was round and big at eight months pregnant, about the size of a small watermelon, and my ankles were swollen as I sat on the bed with my daughter. My heart dropped to the floor as she tell parts and pieces of what happened. Once the conversation was over, I immediately called Joe on the phone and questioned him. He denied everything and said it was "all just lies" and he "would never touch her because she is my step-daughter." My world was turned upside down and I could barely stand up. Joe was calm and continued to say that he was innocent as I asked him to come home immediately. Once he arrived at home, we talked again and he said, "I will prove my innocence, call the police and I will take a lie detector test."

My purpose for relocating to Atlanta was for the both of us to obtain employment so that we could bring the family closer. Joe would not have to travel away to work and the entire family could attend church together. Things were supposed to be better and the children were adapting to living in a large city, though they missed the family back at home. All this changed when we explored the city and they began making new friends and enjoying the various affordable activities offered in the big city.

Things were going to get better for me and my family. Joe and I were searching for employment. Joe got hired really fast because he's skilled in construction, and in about two weeks I found a temporary job. This was the solution, so I thought, moving to a larger city. The one thing that was missing was that we needed a church home. The Thomases suggested a church in the area we were residing so I checked it out one Sunday.

Apostolic Tabernacle Ministries is a mixed congregation with all kinds of nationalities. The church members included African, Caucasian, Hispanic, Greek, as well as other individuals from around the world. The church service was different from my last two experiences and the first visit was interesting. There was an authentic praise and worship service and the women didn't wear make-up or jewelry unless it was a wedding ring. Everyone was so nice, and when you walked through the doors, you could feel this warmth and a loving spirit. You would be greeted with, "Praise the Lord, my sister" and the biggest smiles and tenderest hugs from the greeters. No one was wearing big hats or glittering dresses or flashy men's dress suits. It was a more casual atmosphere and the people were just there to worship and praise Christ.

There were songs I wasn't accustomed to hearing, however when the choir sang them, it brought tears rolling down my

The Painful Trial

face. There was no one with titles such as Bishop Caterpillar or Evangelist Butterfly like there had been in my previous churches. Titles didn't matter here, and all the focus was solely on God. The spirit of the church was refreshing each time you would walk through the doors. We were new residents in the area, and this was the first church I had visited by the referral from the Thomases. We joined the church and became faithful on Sundays and on Bible study nights. My husband did attend church with the kids in the beginning, but now that he was working two jobs, he gave that as an excuse to not go.

I paused at this comment and thought, "Not this again, we relocated so there could be no excuse." The plan was for the entire family to be active in the ministry. Sisters, it was all planned in my mind as I was trying to make an unholy marriage work without God's approval. I prayed and cried to my God every day, "Lord, touch Joe's mind and make him spend more time in Your presence." It never occurred to me to ask, "Is this God's will, or is it something I wish to happen?" I had questions in my mind all day and all night, and all I wanted was for my marriage to work. We had taken the vow "until death do us part" and I wanted to keep it.

My sister in Christ shared Biblical advice and provided scriptures to meditate on for my marriage. 1 Corinthians 7:14 (NKJV) says, "For the unbelieving husband is sanctified by the wife, and the unbelieving wife is sanctified by the husband; otherwise your children would be unclean, but now they are holy." I kept scratching my head over this scripture and asking the Lord for revelation. I would ask, "What are you saying, Lord? How can I sanctify my unsaved husband?" Remember, my first prayer was, "Lord, send me a sanctified, Holy Spirit-filled husband. Is this the husband to my prayers? Thoughts were racing through my head as I tried to figure out where I went wrong.

I began to look forward to church and getting prayer for my husband and I knew that all things would work out for my good. Months passed. I stayed home from work to go to the emergency room because I wasn't feeling well. The blood work and urine test results came back and the physician walked into the room and said to me, "Congratulations, you are pregnant." I was shocked and speechless. "NOOOOOOOOOOO!" I thought in my mind, "Not now! This is not a good time in my life to bring another baby into this world." Morning sickness was taking such a toll on me that I couldn't stand up for long periods of time. I stopped working, and during my first and second trimester, I couldn't eat heavy foods or stand the smell of garlic and onion powder.

Joe was excited about the pregnancy and continued to support the family by working two jobs. I had mixed feelings about being pregnant and his absence, and that he was not filled with the spirit of God. My spiritual supporter encouraged me to continue to pray and to make an appointment to get marriage counseling. I made an appointment and told my husband that the pastor and his wife wanted to come over and counsel with us on next Saturday. Joe's response was, "I have to work" and he basically just blew me off. My hormones were going crazy and my spirit man was trying to stay positive and walking by faith.

My patience was wearing out fast and I wasn't sure what my next move would be. My husband was refusing to seek God's will and now he completely stopped attending church services. I began pleading with him day and night, asking him to obey the Word of God because he was the head of the house. The more we talked, the greater the strain became on our marriage and my pregnancy. There were no words I could say to my husband to get him to the church house.

"Joe, you need to come home now, the police are here waiting for you to ask questions," was the phone call that I had to make, and shortly afterwards, I fell on my knees weeping, asking the Lord, "Where are you? Why is this happening to me?" My cousin came over and took the kids with her so I could go to the doctor because I was at risk of having the baby prematurely. Joe had been arrested and continued to deny doing anything wrong. Mentally and emotionally, I was all over the place, and my doctor told me to get some rest and take it easy. The devil's voice was ringing in my ears all this time saying, "You are serving your God, where is your God now? Was it worth you going to church service Sunday and Tuesday night to serve your Lord now?"

This was my place of Lo-Debar. I couldn't hear from God and there was no communication from heaven during this great trial. My spirit man was heavy feeling as though I was having an out of body experience. My mind was trying to slip away, however because I was due to have my unborn child in weeks, I could not lose my mind, my kids needed me. I fought to hold my tears back in front of the children and tried to stay strong, and while my kids where asleep, I talked and cried to the Lord for at least three months straight. Have you ever cried so many tears that you didn't have any tear drops left?

My husband had been arrested and now iam a single mom trying to raise my children on my own. I was only working part-time, therefore Joe made the most money and paid all the bills. The family attended counseling to cope with this major life switch. My teen daughter received one-on-one counseling and we all took part in group therapy. Family members were saying that my daughter was going to be miserable and promiscuous and that she would not be able to enjoy a normal life. My faith was in the Lord concerning my daughter and there was nothing too hard for my Lord. At the writing of this book, my daughter is happily married to her high school sweetheart who is the only man she had an intimate relationship with (just testify). Don't allow people to plant negative thoughts in your life. Believe that God is in control.

My water broke while sitting in the doctor's office. The medical nurse checked my cervix and I had dilated four centimeters. He intended to call the ambulance, but I didn't have my luggage with me. I was with my teen son and I promised the doctor that I'd go straight to the hospital when I left the office. Snowflakes were coming down in small patches now and I was on my way to deliver my baby. I made sure food was at the house and everyone was safe and my son said, "Mom, I am going to be with you, don't worry." He could tell I was sad because my husband would not be a part of our daughter's birth. We arrived safely at the hospital and I had been assigned a labor room. "Push! Push!" the nurse screamed, "Now one more time, give us a big push." Soon I heard the baby crying in the background, and a voice said, "It's a healthy girl."

Some of my co-workers came to take us home from the hospital. The doctor would not allow me to drive my car. My other kids were excited to see their new baby sister and shouted, "Momma's home!" At the apartment, as we began adjusting to the new living situation, reality kicked in that I was the head of my household. My children played in the snow and were taking turns holding the new baby sister. The rent and other bills were past due, and my bank account was overdrawn. I must start back to work to pay my bills. The doctor released me after six weeks and I started back to work. One Sunday morning, we were on the way to church services, but my six-month-old baby girl was not feeling very well. I thought she might have been teething, so I gave her liquid fever medication for babies. We were sitting in the church services and the baby was crying and her body began to shake, and her eyes roll back into her eye sockets. I was in shock. I didn't know what was going on with my baby. The young minister came and took the baby and me to his office and began to pray while a sister called

The Painful Trial

the paramedics. He laid hands on my baby and looked at me and said, "She is healed by the blood of Jesus" (just testify). She is now a healthy young adult and ever since the young minister laid hands on my daughter, the seizure stopped immediately and never came back. Praise God!

The bills were overdue now and my check would not cover all my bills, but I continued to pray to God to help me. I asked, "Lord, how will I make it through? The bills are overdue, and the rent is late. God, where are You? Are You there?" My husband was sitting in jail, and I was out working to pay the bills and taking care of the children. I had to find a place to stay and I wasn't sure where to go. I was told by a lady I met at the supermarket that she had to stay in a shelter for three months and she was given a section eight voucher. I was thinking maybe me and the kids could stay in a shelter home for women and could get free rent assistance, but the Lord proved to me that He could supply all my needs. A single mother with five kids and a newborn baby with nowhere to go, and the Lord made a way (just testify).

I was on my knees every day and every night praying to God and asking, "What can I do?" I received a promotion on my job with a huge raise. God blessed me and the kids with a big, nice, spacious home and gave me favor with the property manager. She asked if I could pay $1,300 hundred a month but it was a too steep for me. I went back down on my knees and said, "God, Your Word says, 'Ask and it shall be given,… knock and the door shall be opened.' If it's Your perfect will, let it be done." Praise God, we moved into the home and the rent was adjusted to my requested amount. Won't He do it if we ask Him to? (Just Testify.)

Living a single life with a new baby was not easy, however with God on my side, I could make it. I was working in my new position, however childcare for the baby was needed. What would I do? I fell down on my knees and talked to God about the situation. I was led to stop by a nursery near my house and went in and spoke to the owner. Mrs. Kent and her husband had owned this daycare for years and I told her about my situation. She told me to apply for childcare assistance and I followed the advice. Weeks went by while I was waiting for DFACS to approve the application. Mrs. Kent called me and asked if I had heard anything about the childcare application. I responded with a "nothing." She said, "Bring the baby and the other children, and don't worry about the payment. I will provide before and after school care for the pre-school and free daycare for your baby. The favor of God was raining over my life like never before.

Another year came and was gone. My husband was deported from the States. God began to speak to me and told me, "Your husband was hindering your blessings because of your disobedience of being unequally yoked and not seeking My will. You had to endure hardship. You will experience blessings like never before and my Word shall come to pass in your life."

God knew this trial was coming and He positioned me in the right place. The Holy Spirit revealed that the baby was placed in my womb to keep my mind. All mothers can agree that when you have children and are preparing for a new baby, your mind must be on the welfare of the kids.

Many times, it's not the enemy who brings on trials in our lives, but our disobedience that will delay our blessings. When you know to seek God's purpose and ignore it, be ready to face tribulation. Jeremiah 29:11 (NKJV) says, " For I know the thoughts that I think toward you, says the Lord, thoughts of peace and not of evil, to give you a future and a hope." Please understand, Saints, we can't change the course the Lord has on our lives. As you have read thus far, I was the one that chose to relocate. I wanted my family to attend church together, I wanted my husband to attend church, however did I seek what God wanted for me? Are you

The Painful Trial

requesting, seeking, or demanding something from the Lord? God does not move with our demands, because He didn't tell us to demand. Saints, we must always seek the will of our heavenly Father regardless of the situation.

As you have read, my wayward spirit brought difficult times, therefore, my children had to suffer a great deal. A Mother's love for her children causes her to not wish for the them to suffer pain. Yes, we all have trials and tribulations, but my point is that obeying God will provide comfort, and staying in the will of God will ensure your offspring will receive the promise of God. Pause for a moment and reflect on the children of Israel, when they were in the wilderness for forty days because of their disobedience and the older group didn't make it into the promised land.

Take time to study the book of Exodus and find the reason why the Israelites lacked belief and delayed the promises of God. The story of Moses revealed his disobedience, and this caused him not to enter the promised land. Envision walking in Moses' shoes right now and think of all he had to endure over and over again, but just one thing he did wrong resulted in him not taking part in the promised land. Will you be the next Moses? Or are you a Jonah? Friend, we can make this journey by obeying and trusting God to bring us out.

Overcoming Singleness

I would like you to be free from concern. An unmarried man is concerned about the Lord's affairs—how he can please the Lord. - 1 Corinthians 7:32, NIV

Spiritually naked and alone with no ministry to attend, I was living life as a single parent, working and taking care of the children. There were happy days, and there were lonely days. I had left the church and had no spiritual covering, but this lifestyle was not good for my spirit man nor for my well-being. "Spiritually naked" is a term we hear mainly in sermons however, I believe that it means that we are exposed to the enemy with no protection. When we leave God's presence, it places us in a dangerous position. A spiritual covering protects the Saints because we have an assigned watchman to pray, alert, and warn us of hidden dangers. The shepherd watches over the sheep and is held accountable by God to provide protection for the Saints. Romans 10:14 (NKJV) says, "How then shall they call on Him in whom they have not believed? And how shall they believe in Him of whom they have not heard? And how shall they hear without a preacher?"

We hear people quote Bible scriptures all day long, however we need to live the scripture. Days went by when I was working a full-time job and focusing on my master's degree. Even though I was no longer a member of a church, I knew how to talk to God. I was seeking and believing our Father in heaven would send my husband so I wouldn't feel lonely, and the Holy Spirit spoke the Word, "But seek first the kingdom of God and His righteousness, and all these things shall be added to you. (Matthew 6:33, NKJV).

I can recall many nights of praying, crying, and fasting—pleading to God for my "Boaz," as the church mothers would say it, to no avail. It didn't happen, and my life felt void in many ways. Let me share a little history about my marriage. I really did love my husband, and though we had tough times, married life was great. Joe was the first man I had ever felt this way about before and it was challenging for me to walk away from the sin. In the past, I had been able to dodge and remain off the radar because the Holy Spirit had a shield over my life.

How do you know when the Lord places a shield of protection on your life? One of the ways I knew was because of a situation in which the Holy Spirit's protection was evident in my life. There was a nice, handsome, male co-worker on my job who would be flirty with me. Of course, you know it felt really good. I can recall him standing near the gym and he and I would smile at each other. One day we switched numbers, however, he would never call. It appeared that each time I would meet a nice handsome man it was like there was a fear on their face. I began to think to myself, what is wrong with me? Am I ugly? And why are the guys afraid?

The voice of the Lord spoke saying, "I have to protect what I have placed in you."

This got my attention and I asked the Lord, "What are you protecting?" The Lord spoke again and said, "I can't allow your spirit to get contaminated." After this conversation with God, it gave revelation.

Back to where we left off, what did Joe have that other men didn't have? One thing I liked about Joe is that when we would get into arguments, he would always stay quiet and many times he would take his car keys and say, "I am going to let you cool off and I will be back." When he did return to the house, he would say a joke like, "You know I am sexy and irresistible." I would try my best to keep a frown on my face, but he could always make me laugh, even when I was frustrated and then it would be make-up moments. Let me get my thoughts together and say, I would think about Joe even after God removed him from my life. Years went by and I would think about my unyoked, failed marriage less frequently.

At work in the classroom, the students and I were talking about God. Although, we were not sure who started the conversation, the students began asking me religious questions. One young male teenager walked up to me after class and invited me to visit his church and gave the name and the location. By this time, I had already backslid from God and began to attend social networking gatherings with a co-worker. It was not a dating service or a party, but it was created by collegial associates for alumni to meet and greet each other at various five-star restaurants in Atlanta. I was sitting at Lenox grill restaurant in Buckhead socializing with people from various places around the globe. At the bar, I struck up a conversation with a guy and we talked for two hours. He was from Canada and was staying at the Ritz Carlton hotel. An attractive Canadian fashion designer with beautiful, short, curly hair, a very interesting, handsome man.

He invited me back to his hotel, however I turned down the offer and we parted ways. Now there was an African American guy that had been staring at me from across the bar. He approached and asked if he could sit and talk and we talked for hours as well. A well-mannered true Renaissance man who was born in the poor areas of Atlanta, joined the military, worked on Wall Street, and played professional football. A multimillionaire who has a very nice, strong built man who weighed about 260 pounds and was 6'4" inches tall. Wow, his physic took my mind away and we swapped numbers and began to talk. Tony and I began to meet at various five-star restaurants in Atlanta. He was truly a wine and dine man who pays the bill. We were attracted to each other and he was a very intellectual and brilliant man. When he talked, it was like talking to an encyclopedia. The temptation was very strong, and it was hard for me to resist and guess what? I could no longer resist and we began to see each other on a regular basis. Now when Tony and I first met, I shared with him about the ministry on my life. Tony would say I made him nervous, nevertheless, we continued to meet when he would return from traveling. Tony travelled globally as a financial analyst for global fortune five hundred companies and private organizations. The devil knows who to send into my life and I was caught off guard. The Holy Spirit was speaking and the guilt of sinning would not allow my spirit man to rest. I had to make a decision. Tony offered to put me on his payroll and said, "Let me know if there is anything you need, and I will give it to you."

God is the head of my life and I couldn't live an unholy life, so I turned down his offer and explained to him that I have ministry to fulfill. The Holy Spirit led me to tell Tony he also has a high calling on his life and this man knew the Word of God. I visited my student's church on a Sunday and the presence of the Holy Spirit filled the sanctuary. As the months went by, I began to show up to this church every Sunday and finally was led to become a member.

The church singles ministry was a great opportunity to fellowship with other sisters in Christ who had something in common with myself. We met and participated in one social activity once a month. Sis Helen and I started a book club and begin to read spiritual books on *Single Living*. Michelle McKinney Hammond, the renowned author and spiritual woman of God writes powerful books to motivate and share her struggles in overcoming singleness with women from around the globe. Ladies, if you are struggling with living the single life, read Michelle Hammond's book *What to Do Until Love Finds You* to open your spiritual eyes. It was like the words on the pages of her book would speak directly to my heart. She shares her struggle on how God chose her to write books to inspire women to stay in the perfect will of God. She has written over 40 books and she serves as a motivational speaker. Praying, fasting, and reading Michelle's books opened my spiritual eyes, and now I am an overcomer of being single. I love my single life because I get to spend more time in the presence of God, but does this mean marriage is not God's will? Seek ye first the kingdom of God and all these things will be added to you. If it's God's will for marriage, it will be done, but I am content at the present time. During my singleness struggle, before my deliverance, God spoke, "Your life is a testimony for others, and I have chosen you for such a time as this."

Jesus knows the struggles we will face with being single and He assured the Saints that we are overcomers. Many sisters have shared with me about the loneliness and the intimacy of not having a mate, however, it's critical for us to keep our flesh under control. I will share my secrets on how I was able to keep my flesh in subjection with the help of the Holy Spirit. 1 Corinthians 9:27 (NKJV) says, "But I discipline my body and keep it under control, lest after preaching to others I myself should be disqualified." Celibacy is much easier when you don't allow room for temptation. For myself, I would not hug a man, but shake his hand instead, regardless if he is a saved, satisfied holy man or a single attractive "Lamman Rucker look-alike." It didn't matter. I would meet only in public and explain before going out to lunch or dinner, no hugging or kissing on the checks. In fact, there was one guy I would talk to on the phone, and meet at different restaurants. We knew each other for over three years. He knew I was celibate, saved, and sanctified, however, the rules were, no hugging, touching, or kissing on the checks. Sisters, why would you allow a man to hug and touch you to wake up your flesh? Keep in mind that the man who you think is your mate has a soul and God is going to hold you accountable for sharing the gospel of life. There have been many times when I would meet a single guy that God was using me to plant the seed, though I didn't know it at the time.

Once during my undergrad year, I met this handsome guy called "G" and he and I would hang out together at the movies. I invited "G" to church, and he would say to me, "I am too nervous to come and I am not ready to give up my beer." We both graduated, and he went one way and I went another. A year later, I was out in the community and I heard a man calling my name and it was "G." He said to me, "I am saved and filled with the Holy Spirit!" I thought, "Unbelievable," and all this time in the past I was thinking he would never attend church. God knows the plan (just testify). "The wages of sin is death," and is sex worth losing your soul? Wake up and stand strong and learn how to be in control over your mind which controls the flesh

The Oil of Gladness

You have loved righteousness and hated wickedness. Therefore God, your God, has anointed you with the oil of gladness beyond your companions. - Psalms 45:7, ESV

For the oil of gladness has been poured on the sons and daughters of Zion. The oil sets us apart for the service of the Lord. You have the oil dripping from you and others around can see it on your life.

Recommitting to God was the beginning of spiritual maturity for me, and it allowed my eyes and heart to be opened to hearing God clearly. A fresh anointing and a spirit of obedience became my priority, and the Holy Spirit was teaching all things and reminding me of everything. My spirit man was hungry and thirsty for the Word and I was searching for answers.

I purchased a book entitled *Purpose Driven* by Rick Warren and began to read it with conviction. It was like the Holy Spirit was speaking to me and providing directions and answers. I was asking questions like, "Lord, why am I here on this earth? What is my purpose, and after reading this book, will my entire life change for the greater?" I made highlights and scribble notes on each page and poured over every word. During this time in my life, I had many trials and survived them all.

I was at Bible study praising and worshiping on a Wednesday night, and the Spirit moved mightily. When I arrived home, I tried to call my oldest son, but he was not responding to my phone calls. The next day I got a knock on the door and a young boy and his mother told me, "Your son was arrested last night." I immediately drove to the jail and was told that my son was being charged with armed robbery. My heart dropped because all these years I prayed and with the grace of the Lord, my son had never been in a jail cell. He was only sixteen years old and the first visit was difficult for me. My son was sitting on the other side of the glass and we talked on the phone to each other. I noticed a slit in his throat and tears began to run down my face. He said, "Mom, don't cry. I will be alright, just continue to pray for me."

Saints, this was too hard for me to bare and I contacted my pastor to get spiritual counsel. In my mind I was thinking, "Lord why? He is still my baby and he is only 5 feet and has a small built frame. How will he survive in prison?" My pastor gave me spiritual advice and told me to keep the faith and know that God was still in control. He reminded me to trust in the Lord and be encouraged. A year later, he was sent off to a maximum-security prison, however the Spirit of our heavenly Father gave me internal peace. My son served seven years in prison and God kept him safe (just testify) until he was eventually set free, and it's all due to the glory of the Lord. God brought me through the painful tribulations of hurt and mental failures. He made me an overcomer and it's all because of His glory.

I was no longer living as a backslider and had fully committed to serving my Lord with my whole heart, body, and soul. There is a very old Christian song that says something like, "Don't straddle the fence" which clearly means we can't serve two masters because we will always hate one and love the other. My former supervisor would say, "The choice is yours, my friend." The saved and the unsaved often think that the true meaning of our existence is only to achieve personal fulfillment, however we are created to please and to serve our heavenly Father. Jesus was not selfish and always put others before his own needs. He was a true model on how the Believers should live on this earth.

Now that I had matured in the things of the Lord, I was in a position to hear from God, but I wasn't sure how I would hear from Him. I wondered, "What does His voice sound like? Does God talk to His children?" I was on my knees praying every night, asking for Him to reveal my purpose on this earth. Sin can keep us from hearing and receiving the promises of the Word. We must turn away from sin and run to our Redeemer. I began to see answers to my prayers and doors began opening for me. Have you ever heard the voice of God and you second guessed it and said, "No, that wasn't His voice"? This was a season in my life, and it was like having a battle in my mind.

Looking back to when I was living single and searching for a house to lease for me and the kids, I remember one day when I drove through a neighborhood with huge homes, and in my mind I thought, "Wow, one day we will be able to live in a big home." The house was for rent and the property manager met with me and she said, "If you want the house, it's yours." The home was approximately 3,000 square feet which included five bedrooms, three full baths, an extra room, a huge family room, a dinner room, a sunken den, a master bedroom with a fire place, two full walk in closets, a master bathroom with a jacuzzi bath tub, and a kitchen with a double garage. The master bedroom was so huge that I had a king size bed set, sofa, chair, coffee tables and end tables. A workout area with a desk and study and it had more room. "Delight yourself in the Lord, and he will give you the desires of your heart" (Psalms 37:4, ESV).

Single ladies, take note, you don't need a husband to get the desires of your heart for you. The key to reaping the promises of God is to seek first His kingdom. The single ministry at the church allowed the sisters to encourage each other and to share one another's experiences, however, I have heard things such as, "I can't wait for God to send my Boaz so I can travel." "I need my Boaz to buy my dream car." You don't need a man before you can fulfill your dream to travel. Put aside your money and plan a vacation and take a friend or your family on vacation and live your life *now*. Ephesians 3:20 (NKJV) says, "Now unto him who is able to do exceeding abundantly above all that we ask or think, according to the power that work in us."

We don't need a husband or a man in our lives to be happy and enjoy life. Take a deep breath ladies, if a woman desires to get married, it's okay to just wait for the Lord to send him. Better yet, ask God if it's His desire for you to have a mate. If you have the anointing of God over your life and he has given you the faith to believe and confess, then it will come to pass. Meditate on the Word of God and study it. The more you stay in the Word, the more you exercise your faith and you will experience the manifestation of the promises.

How to Hear from God by Joyce Meyer is the book I purchased to provide spiritual guidance. The spirit man is hungry and thirsty for the Word of God; the Holy Spirit will instruct you as you read material written by other spirit-filled Christians. "Here I am," Samuel answered as he ran to Eli. "Did you call me Eli?" asked Samuel. "I didn't call, go back and lie down," replied Eli.

"Samuel," the voice called out again, Samuel went to Eli a second time. "Did you call me?" Eli replied. "I didn't call. Go back and lie down." The voice of the Lord called out again, "Samuel." Samuel ran to Eli and said. "Here I am," and by this time, Eli realized the Lord was calling the boy and said, "If he calls out your name again, say, "Speak Lord, for your servant is listening."

During my communication with God I allowed the Spirit to have His way. Many times God is speaking to us, however we are too busy on the cell phone with broken down Joe, or on Facebook talking about the tight dress Sister Blue wore to church, or maybe we are watching "The Albania House Wives." The voice of God does not sound like the Allstate man who does the commercial, however His voice is a still small voice and when your everyday life is noisy, you will not hear His voice. Joyce Meyers stresses a personal relationship is not a religion and the Saints must get into a quiet place to hear what God is saying to us in these last days. God may send people into our lives for a season to aid us with this spiritual walk and we must take heed to say, "Speak Lord, for thy servant is listening."

It was a great accomplishment for me when I received a confirmation from the University saying, "Congratulations on receiving your Master of Education degree, a job well done." (Just Testify.) Do you remember when I stated at the beginning of this book that it was not my desire to attend a college? However, if you have been following as I have shared my journey with you, I continued to move forward in my studies with the grace of God. For all of my readers, no matter what you have experienced in the past, it may have been a divorce, the death of a spouse, molestation, the loss of a job, being laid off from work, or external factors such as recovering from drug addiction, mental illness, alcoholism, an ex-offender, whatever it may be, you have a *purpose* and a *calling on your life*! "Be not weary in well doing." God is raising you up for "such a time as this." All that you have been through or are going through is for God's glory. The tears, the pain, the hurt, and the suffering is not in vain. Stand up! You have been chosen and equipped to stand against the wiles of the enemy.

Trials come to make us stronger. When you are an overcomer, your victories are not for selfish reasons, however they are for you to pass the mantle on to the next person who is going through or may have to go through the trials that you have, because our Father raised you as a "chosen one." My life is my testimony and it has not been easy, nor did I expect it to be. Have you ever heard people pray, "Lord, make ministry easy"? When did we read Paul stating that ministry was easy? Each time I read the scriptures in the new gospel, Paul stated that he is an ambassador in chains. 2 Corinthians 11:23-28 (NIV) says, "Are they servants of Christ? (I am out of my mind to talk like this.) I am more. I have worked much harder, been in prison more frequently, been flogged more severely, and been exposed to death again and again. Five times I received from the Jews the forty lashes minus one. Three times I was beaten with rods, once I was pelted with stones, three times I was shipwrecked, I spent a night and a day in the open sea, I have been constantly on the move. I have been in danger from rivers, in danger from bandits, in danger from my fellow Jews, in danger from Gentiles; in danger in the city, in danger in the country, in danger at sea; and in danger from false believers. I have labored and toiled and have often gone without sleep; I have known hunger and thirst and have often gone without food; I have been cold and naked. Besides everything else, I face daily the pressure of my concern for all the churches."

How many of us have suffered as Paul did for the kingdom of heaven? We have not been beaten for Christ, placed in prison for Christ, starved almost to death for Christ, or shipwrecked for Christ. The Christian walk is nothing to take lightly. We can say with our lips every day that we love God, but are we willing to give up our lives for God? There is need for a wakeup call for us Saints. There are Believers around the globe that are being persecuted every day for living for Christ. When persecution comes to your door, what will you do?

Finally, I have matured enough spiritually that I have found inner peace and I am no longer crying and praying when I am faced with difficult circumstances. I am able to fall on my knees and pray, and when my faith is challenged, I cast all my burdens on the Lord. Stay in the perfect will of the Lord and watch your life change for the greater. Block out the distractions and get into a quiet place to hear the voice of our Savior. No one has known the time or the hour when the Son of man will appear. Be encouraged my friend and know that the Word of Jehovah is coming to fruition.

Discovering My Purpose

"For I know the plans I have for you," declares the Lord, "plans to prosper you and not to harm you, plans to give you hope and a future." - Jeremiah 29:11, NIV

A quiet, still voice spoke and revealed my calling during one of the most uncomfortable seasons in my life. Now my normality is authentic and my intimate spiritual relationship with God is growing. The more time I spent in the presence of the Spirit of God, the greater the commission became on my life. Luke 12:48 (NKJV) says, "But he who did not know, yet committed things deserving of stripes, shall be beaten with few. For everyone to whom much is given, from him much will be required; and to whom much has been committed, of him they will ask the more." Saints, we must remember that there are spiritual levels of prayer and to experience each level will require more than you have done before, such as fasting and listening to the voice of God. In my secret closet I often pray,

"Lord, use me and get glory from my life, I want to be real in my walk with You." My everyday life was noisy and busy, such as taking my children to school, working, attending college, and taking care of my mom. The voice of God was speaking; however, it was hard for me to hear. One day, I was driving my car with my two daughters and the baby girl was sitting in the back asleep. The light was red and as I waited to make a right turn, I heard a loud BANG and felt a hard jerk in my body. Immediately I looked over at the girls to check on them. The off-duty police officer had hit the rear of my car and then got out of his car to ask if we were ok. The police officer's insurance carrier refused to pay for my pain and suffering and this left the family without having a car for six months.

I prayed to God and asked for my car to be repaired, however God delayed the car repair and held up my case for six months. The first attorney working on the accident case refused to continue the case and I had to search for another lawyer. This was a challenging time for me, and it was hard for me and the kids not having transportation, however I didn't know yet that God was working on my behalf. We walked a total of four miles a day on school days to take my baby girl to school and pick her up, and she was not happy because the winter was very cold.

First the car accident, no car, and no way to get to work, but God provided for my family (just testify). God was talking to me and He had to block all the distractions so I could hear His voice. After taking my daughter to school in the morning, I walked into the house, took out my Bible and began to pray. One day, while praying, I heard the Spirit of the Lord say to me, "Pray for my people." In my mind, I was already praying, so I thought. Then the voice of the Spirit of God said to me, "Pray for the souls of my people." A third time the voice of the Lord said to me, "high calling" and I was puzzled for a long time, trying to figure out what this meant. By this time, I was attending a church every Sunday and going to every Bible study. The voice of God said to me, "You are my chosen, and you are called to intercede for my people."

I am an intercessor and now the voice of the Lord was telling me to pray for His people. The voice of the Lord said again, "Intercede for the pastor and the members." God was talking and I was talking back to Him. "Lord, why do you want me to be the intercessor for the people? And besides, the pastor already has an intercessor." The voice of God spoke again, "You are my chosen, and I want you to intercede for the souls of my people."

Now remember when I mentioned earlier that there are levels of prayer and in order to mature to each level there is a spiritual condition that it will require? Many of us know how to pray things like, "Lord, bless me with a brand new car," or, "Father, bless me with a new home." Yes, this is praying, however this is not spiritual warfare prayer. Let me explain what I mean. The Word says "For our fight is not against flesh and blood, but against principalities, against powers, against the rulers of the darkness of this world, and against spiritual forces of evil in the heavenly places" (Ephesians 6:12, MEV). In order to be overcomers, we must understand how to pray prayers that destroy demonic forces. Spiritual warfare prayer is done by praying in the spirit because the Holy Spirit intercedes with words in heavenly language.

I asked the Lord to teach me how to intercede and to pray for His people. When the police officer hit me from behind, this was divine intervention. In my mind, I was thinking that the devil caused this to happen, but I later realized that God allowed it to happen so I could spend this time with Him. During these six months, my relationship with God deepened and the voice of the Lord would say, "Write this down." And I began to pray for the will of God.

James 4:3 (Version) says, "You ask and do not receive, because you ask with wrong motives, so that you may spend it on your pleasures." What does this scripture really mean? Seeking God's perfect will is our time to discover our purpose on this earth and to learn His plans for our lives. Praying carnal prayers will not cause the blind eyes to open, the dead to rise, or the lame to walk. Jesus didn't pray selfish prayers like, "Lord, kill my enemies, and destroy those who oppose me." As true sanctified Saints continue to mature in the Spirit, our advocate will teach us to bless those who try to come against us. Pray for the co-worker on your job who seems to purposely make your job difficult every day. Pray something like the following: "Lord, bless my enemies. Save them and fill them with the Holy Spirit. Lord, give them a 'Damascus Revelation' as You did Paul, for You are able to do exceedingly abundantly above and beyond all we can ask."

Days went by and I was reading and meditating, and the Spirit of the Lord was revealing spiritual things to me. I recall telling the Lord, "Fill my lips with Your Word. You did it for Moses and You are not a respecter of persons." I asked Him to allow my prayers to be so potent that it would cause immediate actions from heaven. The Holy Spirit began teaching me and talking with me. I was reading the Bible, and other spiritual books.

Now I was not copying from others because when God has anointed you for a purpose, you will not have to take from others and copy. In the Bible, we read and study the words of the disciples of God. Paul didn't try to copy from Peter nor did Simon try to copy from Luke, but each individual had their own spiritual gift and used it according to the Word of God. We have all been uniquely created by God in His own image, therefore, we are not competing against one another, but we are all on the same team. We have shaped each other in our spirit's by walking with one mind, as one body in Christ Jesus.

Discovering My Purpose

I began to listen to the voice of our Father each day and I continued to mature in God's perfect will. My life and my walk with God was aligning with the Word of God. You also have a high calling on your life, and there has been trial after trial to try to distract you from your great destiny, but the blood of Jesus is on your life. I speak no more delay, but now is the time for you to get into the place of holiness and seek God like never before. You will not give up nor give in but "press toward the mark for the prize of the high calling" (Philippians 3:14, Version). You are a "tree planted by the rivers of water" which CAN'T be uprooted by any demon or devil in hell (Psalm 1:3a, Version). Even though you may be tossed and blown, you are an overcomer. You will seek the kingdom of God and the blessings and fulfill your divine purpose on earth. Obey God, my sister. Obey God, my brother. Obedience is the key to hearing from God and seeing the manifestation of His hands on your life.

Our minds will try to play tricks on us if we don't keep our mind on things above. When the Holy Spirit revealed to me that I was an intercessor, the enemy tried to make me believe I was not hearing from God. There were many times when the voice of the Lord would speak, and I was second guessing if it was me or the voice of the Lord. We have to continue to stay in the presence of God and meditate on the Word. Allow the Holy Spirit to give you rest in your spirit.

One Sunday, I was visiting a local church and a sister in Christ walked up to me and whispered in my ears, "God wants you to rest in Him." Days went by and I began to pray in the Spirit and ask God to teach me how to rest in Him. "What does it mean to rest in the Sprit?" you ask. It means to relax, trust God, and allow Him to guide your walk with Him each day. When God speaks to you and nothing seems to happen immediately, don't get agitated but continue to obey. His Word will come to pass, however, we don't have to become impatient and frantic while waiting.

Remember, stay in a place where you can hear from God, and surround yourself by those who are living holy lifestyles. Stay connected with the Saints, those who can pray for your divine purpose to be revealed and the Word of God to manifest in your life.

Walking in my Destiny

For he will complete what he appoints for me, and many such things are in his mind. - Job 23:14, ESV

Blessings are all falling down from heaven because I am obeying the Word of the Lord and living the Scriptures. Have I always been obedient in my walk with God? No sir, it has been very trying and difficult at times, but when God is for you, who can be against you? There were times when I would become weary in well doing. The Word clearly states, "Let us not be weary in well doing"(Galatians 6:9a, KJV). I would thank God every day for His grace and mercy and praise Him for keeping my mind and not giving up on me when I was disobedient.

Some of us don't purposely try to disobey but during our walk we are not viewing the situation through spiritual eyes. Many times, God would instruct me to do something, and one day I heard the heavenly Spirit say to me, "Enroll in a school of ministry." I was still in a secular college working on another master's degree by this time. I said to the Lord, "If this is Your will, send me to the seminary of Your choice." Three years later I was working for a new organization, and during a conversation with Dr. Brown (a co-worker who shared her testimony) she invited me to her seminary college. I visited the college and enjoyed the fellowship with the Saints, however the professor at this location had to relocate due to family issues. This door closed, so then I talked to God and said, "Well Lord, what do You want me to do now? The doors are closed at this location." And we all know when one door closes, a greater door opens for the Saints.

Dr. Brown directed me to another school in Atlanta, GA which was under the same seminary. I visited and knew in my heart that this was the place the Lord wanted me to complete my ministerial studies. My professor and the other students were all living for God and seeking His perfect will, and it was like having another spiritual family. We prayed, supported, and encouraged each other with wisdom and spiritual knowledge. I enrolled in the Doctrine of Ministry program and enjoyed gaining the new material. As I continued my walk with Christ, His favor in my life was so palpable that others around me could see it. My circle of friends allowed me to stay in the perfect will of God and to continue to obey His Word.

Doors opened and doors closed, and I was content because I knew God was in control. My prayer life was evolving, and I was asked to join a prayer line in a local ministry. The Saints were on the line interceding for the souls of God's people. I was attending Women's Conferences and learning more of the Word and networking with shakers and movers for the Kingdom of God. I was asked to speak at a Women's Conference and was walking in the perfect will of the Lord. Now, I was working full time, taking care of my children, and attending the seminary one night a week. We were traveling from state to state, attending and joining in massive kingdom edification. My spiritual mother was a praying woman of God and her faith in the Lord was very strong. I was invited by the pastor to attend the local television station to intercede for the callers.

We were sitting in the prayer room at the station and the pastor asked me to do the live segment, but I declined out of nervousness. It was not because of disobedience, but I was nervous to get up in front of the camera and say encouraging words on live television. When God has pre-destined our purpose, we can't hide or run from the calling. I escaped this time, so I thought. Days passed and I was volunteering one night a week at the local station. On my next visit to the station I was asked again to do the live segment for the prayer line and this time I obeyed. The Holy Spirit led me to the local station to pray for the souls of His people. Now, I had stopped attending the seminary school of ministry due to my work schedule, taking care of the kids, and volunteering at the station.

I was interceding on two prayer lines each week and attending my local church. My faith was being tested and seeking the will of my Father was very critical. We know that obedience is better than sacrifice and with this is a mandate to complete the test. Have you ever prayed and asked God to use you? Often the Saints will cry, pray, and fast to get the Lord's attention, however, when God finally answers, we forget our previous petition.

I was faithful to the church and to praising God and things began to get really challenging. I became distracted by people and things around me and began to lose focus. There was too much disharmony and confusion going on in the church between the Saints and I was trying to seek the Lord's approval to find another ministry. It was a spiritual test, however, I didn't understand why I had to stay in the ministry. The Word says in 1 Corinthians 8:13 (Version), "Be careful not to make my sister stumble." The more

Just Testify

difficult things became, the more I stayed in my secret closet, praying. I asked God, "Why are they being so rude and giving me an evil stare?" After church services, a sister walked up to me and gave me a hug and said these words, "Sister, we can see the anointing of God on your life." The Spirit of God would speak to me and say, "You have purpose here."

I was not a part of a ministry team, however I did volunteer to clean the sanctuary. Ministry is not just doing things in the church that get the pastor's attention, but it's the Great Commission from our heavenly Father to actively spread the gospel to unbelievers. And I am a firm believer in seeking the Lord for answers, and with His guidance, being an auxiliary member of the church ministry. Things began to feel awkward at each service and then one night, God revealed in a dream that witchcraft was present at the church. The pastor preached and confirmed that witchcraft was going on in the ministry. This was the first time I had been led by the Spirit of God to intercede, bind, and loose the jezebel spirit for our members and those who were practicing detestable things in the sight of the Lord.

Church pain can be very frustrating and hard to cope with, however during my tough times, I would praise and pray and then there were other times when I would take a sabbatical from church for months. Now the Word of the Lord came to Jonah saying, "Go to Nineveh, that great city and preach for their wickedness has come up before me." Get this, Jonah tried to run away from the presence of God. Saints, there is no where we can run to escape the presence of God. We must obey, we have no choice. You have a great calling on your life and you must obey God. It's not "all about you." We can't be selfish. Jesus was not selfish, and if we are going to be like Him, we must understand that we are placed on this earth for God's purpose only.

Things got really tough, and the more I interceded, the hotter the fire became, and I became faint. Distraction will take our eyes off of the Lord and we will begin to lose focus. In Matthew 14:29, Peter got off the boat and was walking toward Jesus when he got frightened and began to sink. Saints, we can't get distracted by the things going on around us. We have to trust God in all circumstances and know that He will bring us through. The Lord assigned me to this ministry, and in the beginning, I was obeying and doing great. People joined who were walking in waywardness and began to spread dissension and discord in the Church. Trials came to make the Saints stronger, and during the test, I wanted to run like Jonah. In fact, there were times when I would just stop attending church for months at a time. Each time, I would hear the voice of the Lord saying, "Go back and continue to intercede for the souls."

I can't count the many times I walked in disobedience during this season of my life. This trial made me spiritually stronger and it kept me on my knees, crying and praying and calling on the name of Jesus. My relationship was being strengthened, however, it was not clear why I had to stay and obey God at this particular ministry. The Holy Spirit would say, "It's not about you," And then another day the Spirit of God would say, "It's about the souls of my people." We must learn to see people the way God sees His children.

Finally, after spending long hours in the presence of the Lord, He elevated me to a higher realm. I was able to walk back into the ministry and see souls and not just people each time the Holy Spirit would say, "Pray for the soul." The distractions ceased in my spirit because I had to focus on building the kingdom. How do we stay focused? It comes through staying in the presence of the Lord. Jesus would say to those who tried to distract Him, "I am came to do my father in heaven's will." Saints, this is what it's all about, doing our heavenly Father's perfect will.

Pray, fast, and seek the will of our Savior, and the Holy Spirit will teach you to stay focused. My prayers have changed from when I first began praying. My prayers would be something like, "Lord, send them [the people causing offense] away." However, what I was asking was not God's will. The way The Holy Spirit taught me to pray eventually was, "Lord, save their souls, and thank You. You receive the glory."

Jesus is our example on how to pray concerning His people using the Word of God. I can't remember ever reading in the Bible where Jesus prayed for His Father in heaven to destroy the wicked people, however I have read the Word over and over and discovered Jesus interceding saying, "Father, forgive them, for they know not what they do." Saints, we must come to the place where we can pray for all individuals, regardless of their sinful nature.

A visiting minister preached at my church one day, and he talked about distraction. He taught us that distraction will make the Saints step out of the perfect will of the Lord. Staying in God's will is our protection, and as long we are in the will of our Father in heaven, the protection and blessings continue to flow in our lives from one generation to another.

My graduation day had arrived, and we made it safely to Florida and were preparing for my graduation. I was in pain sitting on the bed and decided to call the twenty-four-hour prayer line. The mother on the other line was reading scriptures and asked if I would start the prayer. She revealed after I had finished praying that she had been feeling ill and once I came on the line and prayed it was like instant healing. We both agreed the virtue of healing manifested on the line early that the morning.

Finally, I received my Doctorate Degree in Ministry (just testify). It took four years to complete the studies at the seminary because, I didn't have my eyes fixed on the Lord and would often lose focus. I would stop and a year would go by and the Spirit would speak and say, "Go back," and I had to obey. When we have been chosen by God for His divine purpose, the Lord will not give us rest until we walk in obedience.

The Victor

God is Spirit, and those who worship Him must worship in spirit and truth. - John 4:24, NKJV

You are chosen and have been commissioned by the Lord to win souls for the kingdom. You have been mandated to spread the good news. What is the good news? The good news is that our Savior lives and continues to release healing and salvation in the lives of His people. The Word of the Lord is sharp and pierces the heart of every man. Mark 16:15 (TLB) tells us, "And then he told them, 'You are to go into all the world and preach the Good News to everyone, everywhere.'" As I mentioned in an earlier chapter, the voice of the Lord spoke to my soul, "You are a testimony for others, and I shall get the glory." Later on in life, the Spirit of the Lord spoke again and told me, "Write a book and I shall get the glory." Five years later, you are holding the book that God gave the title for and instructed me to complete.

Just Testify

During those five years, I would get sidetracked with working, taking care of the family, or attending church, however, the Holy Spirit would not let me rest. I recall the Spirit of the Lord saying, "Just Testify." I started on the book, became preoccupied, and each time the Lord would whisper in my spirit, "The book." There was a moment when I lost the notebook with the information the Spirit had instructed me to write down for the chapters, however I could not find it anywhere in the house. I was talking to God and said to Him, "Lord, I can't find the notebook so what should I do now?" Three weeks later I was cleaning the house and the notebook was found.

My sister and brother, today, if you should hear His voice, don't harden your heart. Obey the Lord, and you shall prosper. I speak no more procrastination, no more delay, and no more doubt into your life. You shall obey the Lord's voice and complete the work He has set before you. The hell you are going through has not been in vain and the Lord shall be glorified. Today is your day to recommit to the task. Your trials were worth it; however, you did not experience trials for you to just sit and tell no one how God can bring you out of them. Jesus' ministry on the earth brought life to the unbelievers as the Word clearly states in John 3:16 (KJV), "For God so loved the world, that he gave his only begotten Son, that whosoever believeth in him should not perish, but have everlasting life"

You may not remember scriptures verbatim, yet there is something God has done in your life. If your family member was delivered from cancer, share this testimony of the greatness of the Lord. In Matthew 8:4 (RSV), Jesus healed the man with leprosy, " And Jesus said to him, 'See that you say nothing to any one; but go, show yourself to the priest, and offer the gift that Moses commanded, for a proof to the people.'" Matthew 9:29 (Version), "The blind men came to Jesus and he healed their eyes and said, 'According to thy faith let it be done.' Jesus said to the men, 'See that no one knows about this.' But they went out and spread the news all over the region."

The hand of the Lord is present on my life, and I could tell you so much that He has done, I don't know where to start. My son has been released from prison and is attending church now. God protected him in prison (just testify). My mother has been healed from thyroid cancer and came through surgery with no mark on her throat from the surgery (just testify). My son-in-law has lupus and was hospitalized with blood clots in his lungs. We prayed for his healing and he has recovered and is off of disability (just testify). My oldest daughter was hospitalized due to a large fibroid with blood clots in her leg and one clot in the lung and had to receive four pints of blood, and she repented of her sin and is healthy (just testify).

The Lord said, "Your faith has made you whole, trust in the Lord not in man." One day, I said to my son, "Wake up, let's go clean out the minivan." The minivan was repeatedly stalling and there were times when the kids and I would get stranded in the middle of the road. This went on for a year or longer. I didn't have any money in my bank account for a down payment on a new car, but I didn't care. My Father in heaven is rich and promised He would open heaven and pour out blessings. So we drove to a dealership and met with a salesman who ran my credit and asked, "How much do have for a down payment?" My reply was, "Nothing" and he said, "What can I do with this minivan that is not resalable?" To make a long story short, we left there with a new car without making a down payment and the salesman paid for the auto insurance and bought lunch for me and my son. This is when you exercise the faith of the mustard seed. I knew what I didn't have, however, I trusted in the Word of the Lord (just testify).

The testimonies above are to share the good news with my readers and those God sends into my life. There is much more, however I will have to leave those to add to future books to be able to list them all. Let me encourage you to *Just Testify* about the goodness of the Lord at your job, to your friends, to your family, and even to your enemies. Study the Word of the Lord and allow the Holy Spirit to teach you and lead you on the straight and narrow way. You may wonder, "What if I make a mistake and fall?" Get back up, repent to the Lord, and He will continue to work in your life. My friend, you don't have to stay in Lo Debar, for the victory is yours today! You are the victor (just testify)!

Behold I have put my words in your mouth, I have appointed you over nations and kingdoms to uproot, tear down, destroy, overthrow, to build and plant. - Jeremiah 1:10, BSB

For information on booking for speaking engagement see contact information below:

Email Address: Justtestifyy@gmail.com
Web address: www.justtestify.org

www.ingramcontent.com/pod-product-compliance
Lightning Source LLC
Chambersburg PA
CBHW071834290426
44109CB00017B/1823